PORTRAITS OF GREATNESS

"Learning Through Stamps"

PORTRAITS OF GREATNESS

"Learning Through Stamps" · Volume 3

By Elizabeth and Klaus Gemming

Barre Publishers

BARRE · MASSACHUSETTS

TITLE PAGE:
William the Conqueror and Norman ships.
France, 1966.

N
5300
.Y4
v. 3

Composition by Barre Publishers, Barre, Massachusetts
Printing by The Lane Press, Inc., Burlington, Vermont
Binding by Sendor Bindery, Inc., New York City
Manufactured in the United States of America

L.C.C. Card No. 68-17069

ABOUT THIS BOOK

THIS IS A BOOK of portraits of great men and women from many centuries, and the portraits, which appear on postage stamps from all over the world, are of many types. There are, for example, self-portraits by Michelangelo, Leonardo da Vinci, and Rembrandt, as well as fine paintings of Martin Luther, Queen Elizabeth I, and Thomas Jefferson. There are unusual engravings, such as the portrait of Vesalius, which was the frontispiece of his famous book on anatomy. From the past hundred years or so, there are of course photographs—portrait photographs of Karl Marx, Winston Churchill, and Eleanor Roosevelt, and candid photographs of such famous people as Albert Einstein, Dr. Martin Luther King, Jr., and John F. Kennedy. There are even caricatures (of Picasso, Hemingway, and Charlie Chaplin)—almost a disrespectful form of portraiture that is, along with the photograph, our own century's favorite way of capturing a personality on paper.

Some of these people died young, and some lived to be very, very old. Many of them were outstanding in several different fields at once. Many were admired and honored in their lifetimes, but a few were virtually unknown for years. Some enjoyed fame and wealth at an early age, but many others lived out their lives in quiet dedication to a cherished ideal.

There are no outright villains in this book, although several of the subjects were not universally respected. In every case, however, these men and women changed the world and left it quite different from the way it would have remained if they had never lived at all. There are gentle and kind people here, and harsh and selfish ones. There are temperamental egotists such as Napoleon and Richard Wagner; modest humanitarians such as Confucius and Pope John XXIII: tormented souls such as Dante and Eugene O'Neill; and heroic figures cut down as they approached the peak of their careers, such as Kennedy and King. Some of these people directly enriched the world for future generations, but others, through acts of tyranny, forced the rest of the world to react nobly to their challenge. Florence Nightingale, for one, inspired people through her own courageous and humane deeds, while Henry David Thoreau quietly and perhaps unintentionally was to inspire men to action two generations later in a much more complex world.

Several centuries ago it was very risky to be a scientist and shake the foundations of faith by questioning the wisdom of the ancient world—yet nowadays we are quite ready to believe anything a serious scientist can reasonably document, without fearing that our entire world will crumble around us. At times in the past, scientists were often outcasts; today they are heroes. In our own busy and practical age it is usually the artists, writers, statesmen, and philosophers who have a harder time.

What will the 21st Century think of the great men and women of today? Some of today's most famous names may merely be recorded fifty years from now. And the most illustrious names from this century may still be unfamiliar to us, although someday they will reserve pages and pages in the history books.

One thing is certain: the giants of history who appear in these pages were individuals—they had almost nothing in common with one another. They differed in education, wealth and family background. They were handsome or homely, cheerful or bitter, generous or jealous. They all had good imaginations and receptive brains, but some achieved success with ease and others hardly sensed their own greatness. Each of these men and women believed sincerely in the worth of their work—religious, political, artistic, scientific—and most of their endeavors were for the good of the world by any standards. Devotion to a personal vision and years of stubborn effort are part of every story.

HORIZONS OF THE OLD WORLD

REPUBLIQUE FRANÇAISE

0.60 CHARLEMAGNE POSTES

BY THE 6th Century A.D. the mighty Roman Empire had collapsed and tribes from the North had overrun the provinces. These "barbarians" (a term that comes from the Greek word for "stranger") settled down and founded a new civilization in Europe. Out of the Dark Ages emerged a noble successor to the Roman emperors, the brilliant, saintly Charlemagne.

Charlemagne (742-814)

Charles the Great, King of the Franks and Emperor of the West, was of Germanic ancestry. He fought many wars to extend and defend his realm and convert the heathen to Christianity. On Christmas Day in the year 800 he was at church in Rome. When he arose from prayers Pope Leo III crowned him "Carolus Augustus, Emperor of the Romans," and founded the vast Holy Roman Empire that was to last more than a thousand years. Charlemagne built churches, palaces, and monasteries, and set up protective "marches" outside the frontiers—one of them was called Denmark. He sent his personal representa-

tives, the *missi dominici*, on regular tours of inspection. His sympathy and concern for all his subjects was unique in his time.

The Emperor himself attended the palace school at Aachen. He spoke Latin and understood Greek but he could read very little and he struggled without much success to learn to write. After his death the great empire fell apart as his sons and grandsons quarreled over his lands. Over the years many legends grew up about the tall, devout ruler, and *trouvères* sang of Charlemagne and his knights, one of whom was the heroic Roland.

William the Conqueror (1027?-1087)

Duke William of Normandy (see title page) was a heavy and fierce-looking man, the grandson of a Norse raider who had settled in the French coastal province. William began to govern at the age of twenty. After the death of the King of England, his cousin, ambitious William sailed across the Channel. At the Battle of Hastings in 1066 the victorious Norman killed the Saxon Harold and became King of England himself. William laid waste much land and imposed high taxes but he was an able and powerful ruler. The culture and language of England were greatly enriched by French influence.

ABOVE: Charlemagne at school. *France, 1966.*

Confucius. *Republic of China, 1965.*

Maimonides. *Spain, 1967.*

Confucius (551-479 B.C.)

This peaceful, tolerant sage lived in an age of banditry and violence. He was a scholar of ancient Chinese literature and a public official who tried to bring about a change of heart among the people. He wandered over China with his disciples for a dozen years, urging local governments to strive for peace and justice. He taught the young to honor their elders. The Golden Rule of Confucius says: What you would not wish done to yourself, do not do to others.

Maimonides (1135-1204)

Moses ben Maimon was born at Córdoba, Spain. He began the study of Greek philosophy and medicine with the best Arab teachers. When the Moors captured Córdoba in 1148, he fled with his parents to Egypt. Eventually he became Rabbi of Cairo and physician to the Sultan. He wrote books in both Arabic and Hebrew. He attempted to codify Jewish oral law, and in *Guide for the Perplexed* he explained many puzzling philosophical and religious questions.

Marco Polo. *Italy, 1954.*

Marco Polo (1254?-1324?)

Marco Polo belonged to a noble Venetian family. When he was about seventeen he left with his father and his uncle on an expedition to China, which was at that time the richest and most highly civilized country in the world. The overland journey took four years. The Polos stayed for seventeen years at the splendid court of the Mongol emperor Kublai Khan. Marco soon became the emperor's favorite and served him as an envoy and a governor. He finally left China in 1292 and reached Venice in 1295 after a journey by sea and land by way of Sumatra, India, and Persia.

Three years later, while commanding a galley in a battle, Marco Polo was captured by the Genoese. During a year in prison he set down an account of his fascinating travels, probably using notes he had once made for Kublai Khan and dictating his story to a fellow prisoner. His book was the first eyewitness account of the fabulous Far East. Two centuries later, daring Portuguese explorers read it, and so did Columbus, who made notes in the margins of his copy.

Marco Polo brought home a wealth of precious jewels from China. He is also believed to have brought some noodles back with him, thus introducing macaroni to Italy.

Dante Alighieri (1265-1321)

The son of a lawyer, Dante was prominent in politics in his native city of Florence. The medieval Italian city-states were torn by hatred and jealousy, and when Dante's party fell from power in 1302 he was banished forever from his beloved town. Lonely and bitter, he wandered from place to place. He died in Ravenna.

Dante. *Russia, 1965.*

Dante was the most learned man of his time. In Latin he wrote a treatise on languages, as well as a proposal for a world empire, *De Monarchia*. In Italian he wrote *La Vita Nuova*, lovely poems telling of his pure devotion to Beatrice, a beautiful little girl he first saw when he was only nine years old.

We know his masterpiece as *The Divine Comedy*, an epic poem that embodies the spirit of the 13th Century. Dante called it simply *Commedia* because it ended happily. The Latin poet Vergil takes Dante on an imaginary journey through Purgatory and Hell, even down to the pit where the devil himself is frozen in eternal ice. Dante meets actual historical persons on the various levels. The blessed Beatrice then leads him through Paradise. For his *Commedia* Dante chose the popular dialect of his native province of Tuscany instead of literary Latin, and, in effect, this brilliant poet created modern Italian.

Gutenberg. *Hungary, 1962.*

Johannes Gutenberg (1398?-1468)

In the 1430's Gutenberg was a metalworker in Strasbourg, making art objects and jewelry, and it may have been there that he invented movable metal type for printing—individual letters of soft lead that could be lined up to form words and pages. By 1448 he had a print shop in Mainz, his birthplace. A goldsmith-partner loaned him the money for a press, but after five years Gutenberg was unable to pay him back, so he had to give up his press, type, and the rights to his invention. Traveling printers quickly spread the use of movable type all over Europe.

Gutenberg, meanwhile, managed to set up shop again. About 1456 he brought out the first book ever printed in the Western world, a Bible. He printed about two hundred copies, with two columns of Gothic type to the page, illuminated by hand. Forty-seven of the Bibles exist today. Gutenberg's name does not appear on any of his surviving work, however, and he died, as he had lived, in poverty.

Leonardo da Vinci (1452-1519)

Leonardo, son of a notary and a peasant girl, was born in the little town of Vinci and grew up in Florence. At fourteen he was apprenticed to the painter Verrocchio. He became court artist to the Duke of Milan, military engineer to the Borgias of Florence, and spent his last years in a French château at the invitation of the King.

He was a restless artist who painted very slowly and left few finished paintings (one of which is the "Mona Lisa"). He was often sued for failing to live up to a contract. His famous notebooks, thirty in all, are written from right to left in mirror-writing—why, no one knows—and are filled with sketches. Among Leonardo's countless interests were: the anatomy of men and horses, the eye, birds, flowers, the dating of rocks, tides, the motion of the planets, rhythm and harmony, stage sets and costumes, military tactics, and

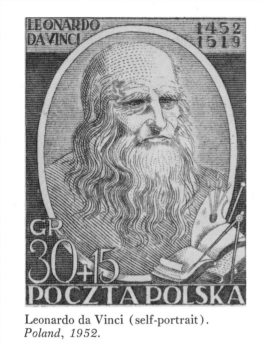

Leonardo da Vinci (self-portrait).
Poland, 1952.

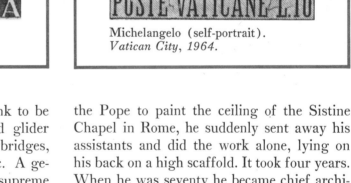

Michelangelo (self-portrait).
Vatican City, 1964.

weapons. He designed an armed tank to be manned by foot soldiers, a manned glider with wings that flapped, a jack, drawbridges, and a plan for two-level street traffic. A genius in every field, Leonardo was the supreme Renaissance man.

Michelangelo Buonarroti (1475-1564)

Michelangelo was of noble birth but his family was poor. He showed so much talent that at fifteen he was invited by the ruler of Florence, Lorenzo de'Medici, to live in the palace and attend the academy there. But after Lorenzo died, seventeen-year-old Michelangelo was on his own. He moved back and forth between Florence and Rome, working for princes, cardinals, and popes. He was quarrelsome and temperamental. Hired by the Pope to paint the ceiling of the Sistine Chapel in Rome, he suddenly sent away his assistants and did the work alone, lying on his back on a high scaffold. It took four years. When he was seventy he became chief architect of St. Peter's, a project long under way, and created the magnificent dome. Bitter and morose, he was still working within a few days of his death, in his ninetieth year.

Michelangelo thought of himself primarily as a sculptor. He worked directly on the stone, believing that a figure trapped inside the marble was struggling to get free. He was considered the world's greatest living artist in an age when all artists were regarded as superhuman geniuses. Michelangelo and Leonardo, the two giants of the Italian Renaissance, disliked each other intensely.

Martin Luther. *Finland, 1967.* The Wartburg. *Germany, 1967.*

Martin Luther (1483-1546)

Luther, son of a fairly prosperous Saxon peasant, began to study law but switched to theology and entered a monastery. Through his Bible study he became convinced that the Scriptures were the only true source of the Word of God. He believed that man could be saved by faith alone, not by good deeds. On a visit to Renaissance Rome he was shocked at the worldly way of life of the "princes of the Church." He formulated some suggestions for Church reform, and on October 31, 1517, he posted on the door of the castle church in Wittenberg his *Ninety-Five Theses*. They were in Latin, intended for debate among monks and professors.

But the theses were quickly translated into German, and printed copies circulated among people of all classes. When the Pope sent a document of condemnation, Luther burned it publicly in the town square. He was summoned before Church and imperial authorities but he refused to give up. The stubborn young monk, who hated violence and had not intended to start a revolution, defied both the Church and the Emperor when he cried, "Here I stand, I cannot do otherwise!" He was formally excommunicated in 1521. The Elector of Saxony, his ruler and protector, hid him for almost a year in the Wartburg, a forest stronghold. There Luther translated the New Testament into German for the first time and began a translation of the entire Bible. His German prose was so forceful that, like Dante's Italian, it helped shape the modern language. In 1525 Luther married a former nun, and they had six children. He was active in establishing a good school system in Germany, and wrote the music for many hymns, including a setting of the Forty-Sixth Psalm, "A Mighty Fortress Is Our God."

Desiderius Erasmus (1466?-1536)

Erasmus, whose Dutch name was Gerhard, was born in Rotterdam. His mother was a doctor's daughter and his father later became a monk. He was a poor boy but he was well educated at a school run by the Brethren of the Common Life, who were the chief religious reformers of the late Middle Ages and the best schoolmasters in northern Europe.

They trained many of the outstanding scholars of the time. Erasmus became a priest and a teacher of Greek, and traveled to England, Switzerland, and Germany. He started his writing career with some funny pamphlets in Latin that described the stupidity of the monks of his day. His humorous works, notably *The Praise of Folly* and *The Education of a Christian Prince* were very popular.

Erasmus edited many Greek and Latin books, including the writings of the Church Fathers. He made the first accurate Latin translation of the New Testament and a corrected edition of the original Greek text. Erasmus and his fellow scholars were called Humanists. They tried to reconcile Christianity with the wisdom of the ancient world, but they were not revolutionaries. They wished to study the Bible in its historical setting and study the Scriptures in the original, and they translated many ancient works into modern languages. Erasmus urged a rebirth of faith and reforms within the existing Church, and he was an outspoken enemy of Martin Luther.

John Calvin (1509-1564)

Calvin, a Frenchman, was learned in the classics, theology, and law. As a young man he experienced a "sudden conversion" and abandoned the Catholic faith. He had to keep moving around to escape punishment, and when he was banished from France by the King he went to Geneva, Switzerland. He was later expelled from there, then welcomed back in 1541. At Geneva he founded a government based solely on strict religious law. He was a stern, unyielding man, intolerant of anyone who opposed him. He preached that the Bible is the only source of God's law and it is man's duty zealously to preserve God's law and order on earth.

Calvin systematized the doctrines of Protestantism and organized its church discipline. The sober Puritans who came from England to Massachusetts in the 17th Century were Calvinists. In both the Old and the New World, the Calvinist virtues of thrift and hard work helped speed up the growth of modern industrial nations.

Erasmus. *Belgium, 1967.*   Calvin. *France, 1964.*

Andreas Vesalius (1514-1564)

Throughout the Middle Ages doctors had relied on the work of the Greek physician Galen. But Galen made many errors because he had dissected only animals. Even in the 16th Century the Church opposed dissection of the human body.

Vesalius, a Flemish-born professor of surgery at the University of Padua, edited Galen's works and challenged many of his claims. In 1543 he published a daring book, *De Humani Corporis Fabrica*, which described human bones, the nervous system, blood vessels, and the structure of the heart—all based on actual dissections. It was illustrated with accurate drawings by a fine artist. The court of the Inquisition sentenced Vesalius to death for his activities, but later modified his punishment to a pilgrimage to Jerusalem. On his way home Vesalius died in Greece.

Gerhardus Mercator (1512-1594)

Gerhard Kremer, known as Mercator, was a Flemish mathematician, geographer, and cartographer. When he was about fifteen he made his first map, a map of the Holy Land. He charted Flanders and made globes of the earth and the heavens. In 1552 he moved to Germany to serve as cosmographer to a duke. He published a six-sheet map of Europe in 1554 and wrote several books on geography and mapmaking. In 1585 he began a great atlas, finished after his death by his son.

The famous "Mercator Projection" dates from 1569. It is a rectangular map of the world with all parallels of latitude drawn to the same length as the Equator. The far north and south are badly distorted because it is impossible to transfer the round earth accurately to a flat sheet of paper, but Mercator's world map has been extremely valuable to generations of navigators and seafarers.

Vesalius. *Belgium, 1964.*   Mercator. *Belgium, 1962.*

Copernicus. *Poland, 1959.* Galileo. *Italy, 1964.*

Nicolaus Copernicus (1473-1543)

Copernicus was born in Poland. He was raised by his uncle, a prince-bishop, and studied in Poland and Italy. He performed many important duties at the Frauenberg cathedral. A devout churchman, he was the first to question the accepted views of astronomy that were based on the orderly universe described by the Greek-Egyptian Ptolemy: heaven was a glassy dome, and the planets circled the earth. Copernicus concluded that the sun, not the earth (nor man, who dwelt on it) stood at the center of God's universe.

His great interest was mathematics, and his theory was not based on actual observation of the stars. He struggled with his ideas for many years and feared condemnation by the Church. His book *De Revolutionibus Orbium Coelestium* was finally published in 1543, the same year as Vesalius's book on human anatomy. Copernicus was gravely ill, and the first printed copy was placed in his hands just before he died.

Galileo Galilei (1564-1642)

Galileo, a professor of mathematics, worked out formulas for many laws of physics. In experiments from the Leaning Tower of Pisa he proved that all falling objects, large or small, descend with equal speed. In 1609 he perfected the first complete refracting telescope and studied the Milky Way, discovered satellites of Jupiter, and observed sun spots. Students from all Europe came to hear him lecture.

With his telescope Galileo also proved that Copernicus had been right, and Church authorities soon warned him about his dangerous ideas. In 1632 he did publish a dialogue stating that the earth moved around the sun, and he was pronounced a heretic, tried, imprisoned, and forced to deny publicly all his claims. Eventually the offended Pope allowed him to retire to a villa in Florence. Galileo's hearing and eyesight were failing but he went on with his experiments until he became totally blind five years before his death.

Queen Elizabeth I. *Great Britain, 1968.*

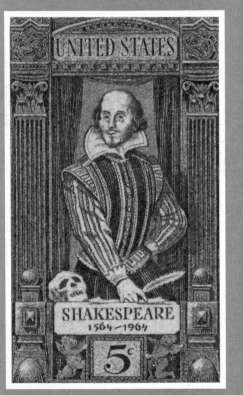

Shakespeare. *United States, 1964.*

Queen Elizabeth I (1533-1603)

Elizabeth was a daughter of King Henry VIII of England. The red-haired princess studied with the best governesses and tutors in the land and succeeded to the throne at the age of twenty-five. England was then deep in debt and torn by religious struggles. Elizabeth had been raised a Protestant, and she ruled that church services were to be held in English, not Latin, and established the Anglican Church with the sovereign as its head.

The young queen, who never married, was vain and stingy, but she chose excellent advisers. She united England and Scotland and defeated England's greatest rival, Catholic Spain. After years of hesitation she had finally consented to the execution of the young and beautiful Mary, Queen of Scots, after discovering plots to assassinate her and place Mary on the throne instead. King Philip of Spain, angry at the English for raiding Spanish ships and for aiding the Dutch against their Spanish rulers, and eager to avenge the death of Catholic Mary, sent out his huge fleet against England in 1588. English and Dutch ships waited off the south coast of Britain. Inspired by Queen Elizabeth's patriotic speech, the daring captains, aided by a severe gale, destroyed the Spanish Armada and broke the sea power of Spain forever. Elizabeth secured a long and stable peace, and the English navy was free to sail the seven seas establishing colonies and trading companies that sent impressive profits home to her beloved England.

William Shakespeare (1564-1616)

Shakespeare was born at Stratford-on-Avon, a busy Elizabethan-English market town. His father was a glovemaker who was active in town affairs, and his mother came from a well-to-do farm family. He went to the Stratford grammar school and may have been a schoolmaster for a while. At eighteen he married Anne Hathaway. They had three children, including twins, but after a few years Shakespeare left Stratford and went to London. He probably started as a stage apprentice and by 1592 was established as an actor and playwright. He won the Earl of Southampton as his patron, was an active member of the Lord Chamberlain's Men, later the King's Players, and earned a good income writing an average of two plays a year and acting in them himself. He bought the largest house in Stratford but continued to live in London. With a group of partners he built the famous and costly Globe Theater on the bank of the Thames, and later the Blackfriars Theater. By 1610 he retired to Stratford with some fortune.

Shakespeare did not bother to invent his own plots but wisely borrowed them from many sources. His incredible output includes appealing comedies such as *A Midsummer Night's Dream*, *The Merchant of Venice*, *As You Like It*, *Twelfth Night*, and *The Tempest;* thrilling history plays such as *Henry IV*, *Henry V*, and *Richard II;* and superb tragedies, among them *Romeo and Juliet*, *Julius Caesar*, *Hamlet*, *Macbeth*, *and King Lear*.

Miguel de Cervantes (1547-1616)

Cervantes was the son of a poor Spanish doctor. As a young soldier he received severe gunshot wounds and lost his left hand in battle. He was captured by Algerian pirates and held as a slave for five years before his devoted family managed to ransom him. After his army service he never found a steady job and he often owed people money. In 1580 he drifted to Madrid and wrote a few plays, none very successful. He tried for a job in South America but was rejected. While he was a tax collector in Granada he served three months in jail for failing to make up a sum that was due the treasury.

While in prison, Cervantes apparently wrote at least part of his great comic novel *Don Quixote*, the story of a poor knight who lived years after the time "when knighthood was in flower." The gentle fellow had read too many romances, and he rode forth to kill giants, rescue fair ladies, and tilt his lance at windmills, all for the sake of a peasant girl. With him rode his squire, Sancho Panza, a country bumpkin. Cervantes made these two absurd characters lovable while he laughed at the out-of-date rules and manners of a bygone age and touchingly brought out the contrast between the real world and the dream world of a well-meaning man.

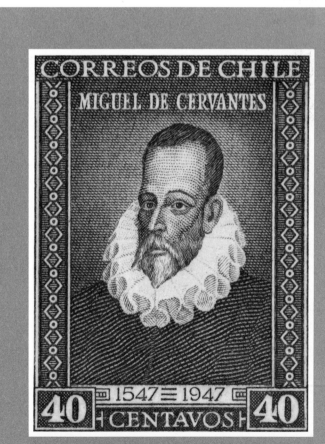

Cervantes. *Chile, 1947.*

Rembrandt (self-portrait). *Bulgaria, 1957.*

Rembrandt painted some sixty self-portraits. The early ones show him young and confident, but the later ones picture a worried man, grieving for his wife and children and worn by poverty. In 1642 Rembrandt was commissioned to paint a group portrait of a volunteer defense company. The portrait was highly original—only a few of the figures were in light and the rest were in the shadows. People were shocked, and nicknamed the painting "The Night Watch." It was a turning point in his career, and by 1656 Rembrandt was bankrupt. A devout Protestant, he worked on Bible scenes and studies of the interesting faces he saw in Amsterdam's Jewish quarter where he lived. His housekeeper and Titus ran a little shop where they sold his work. After both died in the early 1660's Rembrandt lived alone and continued to paint, though his eyes were weak. One of the hardest-working artists who ever lived, he left several hundred etchings, some two thousand drawings, and perhaps six hundred and fifty paintings, many bathed in the golden sunlight that is a special characteristic of his work.

Rembrandt van Rijn (1606-1669)

Rembrandt was the son of a well-to-do miller in the city of Leyden, the Netherlands. While still in his teens he moved to Amsterdam and began working as a portrait painter. In those days Holland, newly free of Spanish rule, was busy and prosperous, and the population was growing fast. There were many plump, wealthy citizens who wanted portraits of themselves in their velvets and furs, and Rembrandt became the most popular painter in Amsterdam. In 1634 he married Saskia, a rich man's daughter, and she brought him money and social position. They bought a large house with studios where he taught many able young artists. But debts began to mount up, and in 1642 Saskia died. The heartbroken Rembrandt was left with a baby son, Titus, and three older children. Only Titus was to live to adulthood.

Bach. *Germany, 1961-64.*

When he died he owned only a few clothes and his painting materials.

Johann Sebastian Bach (1685-1750)

Bach was born at Eisenach, Germany, into a very musical family. Both his father, a violinist, and his mother died when he was nine, and he was raised by an older brother who was an organist. He had little schooling but as a choir boy he loved to copy music and memorize scores in the church library. His first important job was as court organist to the Duke of Weimar. He had already begun a series of organ compositions, and he eventually composed for every known instrument. He married a cousin and they had seven children. By 1717, when he left Weimar to become concert master at the princely court in Cöthen, Bach was regarded as the greatest organist of his time. At Cöthen he led the orchestra and wrote music for concerts. He was humble, industrious, and serious-minded. He read only religious books and his German was ungrammatical—he did not consider himself a genius and neither did anyone else. After his first wife died he married Anna Magdalena, the young daughter of the town trumpeter. She bore him thirteen more children. Bach wrote a charming little book of educational pieces for her.

In 1723 Bach accepted his last job, as cantor of St. Thomas's Church in Leipzig. He was to play the organ at the Lutheran services, train the choir, and direct the performances. The enormous Bach family had to live

Violin and organ. *Austria, 1967.*

in a miserable, cold house, and several babies died. There was little in Bach's life besides overwork, worry, and sorrow, and his genius was both unappreciated and unrewarded. Yet in the years at St. Thomas's he wrote his most magnificent church music: the *St. John* and *St. Matthew Passions*, the *Christmas Oratorio*, the *Mass in B-minor*, and cantata after cantata for specific Sundays. After an operation failed to save his sight, Bach went blind. Just before he died his sight came back, and he worked feverishly to the end, revising and copying his last works.

LIBERTY AND GLORY

Across the Atlantic, in the British colonies of America, people felt a restless desire to be free of the restrictions imposed by the "old country." They wanted to run their own lives, and fortunately, their leaders sensed the thrilling destiny that awaited the New World. The wise and brilliant Thomas Jefferson wrote of the ideals of democracy in the Declaration of Independence: the rights men are born with and can never lose, and the responsibilities of governments to serve well the people who consent to their very existence. He insisted "that all men are created equal, that they are endowed by their Creator with certain unalienable Rights, that among these are Life, Liberty and the pursuit of Happiness."

The idea that all men have the right to live out their lives in safety and dignity, and that governments exist only by consent of the people they govern, was truly revolutionary. The peasants of Europe would not have believed it, and their rulers were not inclined to admit that it might be true.

ABOVE: Jefferson quotation. *United States, 1960.*

Benjamin Franklin (1706-1790)

The Franklins of Boston were a large family—young Ben recalled thirteen children around the dinner table at one time. At twelve he was apprenticed to a printer, and he read every book he could lay his hands on. In 1723 he settled in Philadelphia, where he set up a mutual improvement club, established America's first circulating subscription library, founded an academy that was to grow into the University of Pennsylvania, started a weekly newspaper, and published *Poor Richard's Almanac*.

A witty, common-sense writer, Franklin was also an able scientist. Experimenting with a kite and a metal key in a thunderstorm, he proved that lightning and electricity were the same thing. He was deputy postmaster general for the American colonies and represented Pennsylvania at the first colonial gathering. Back in 1754 he had presented a plan for the union of the colonies, and he helped draft the Declaration of Independence and was one of its signers. He was a popular and effective ambassador to France and negotiated peace with England after the Revolution. In 1787, when he was over eighty, he took an active part in the Constitutional convention.

Franklin. *United States, 1955.*   Washington. *United States, 1967.*   Jefferson. *United States, 1968.*

George Washington (1732-1799)

"The squire of Mount Vernon" was a native Virginian. He was a militia commander on the frontier, and later served in the Virginia House of Burgesses and the Continental Congress. When he took command of the army it was a poorly trained and badly disciplined force. Washington drove his men hard but he was always fair to them, and even in the desperate winter of 1777-78 at Valley Forge his calm patriotism and devotion to his men inspired them and gave them courage. After the Revolution he would accept no payment other than his actual expenses and wished only to retire to his farm. He once remarked that agriculture had always been his favorite pastime.

Washington returned to preside over the Constitutional convention, and was unanimously chosen the first President of the United States in the spring of 1789. He was cheered in every village on the way from his Virginia estate to New York for the inauguration before a joyful crowd at Federal Hall in New York City.

Thomas Jefferson (1743-1826)

Jefferson, third President of the United States, believed that America would be happiest if it remained a rural, agricultural democracy. He encouraged immigration and favored free public education for all citizens. With the Louisiana Purchase of land from France, he more than doubled the size of the United States. An aristocrat himself, Jefferson cared deeply about "plain people" and was opposed to a strong central government that might interfere with individual liberty.

He was well educated in law, philosophy,

Paine. *United States, 1968.*

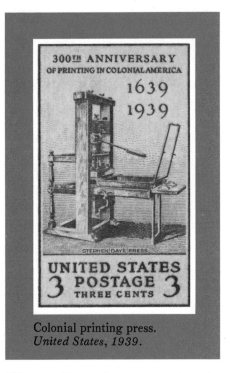

Colonial printing press.
United States, 1939.

science, and music, and owned a large library and print collection. He knew several languages and enjoyed good conversation with people of different backgrounds, whom he often entertained at his gracious home. The "sage of Monticello" was also a gifted architect who designed his own house and the fine buildings of the University of Virginia at Charlottesville. At his own suggestion the inscription on his gravestone lists his proudest achievements: "Here was buried Thomas Jefferson / Author of the Declaration of American Independence / of the Statute of Virginia for Religious Freedom / and Father of the University of Virginia."

Thomas Paine (1737-1809)

Benjamin Franklin met Thomas Paine in England and was much impressed with Paine's fiery revolutionary spirit. Paine arrived in Philadelphia in 1774 with a letter of introduction from Franklin and became an editor and writer of radical political pamphlets. *Common Sense*, published in January, 1776, urged the establishment of an American republic, six months before the Declaration of Independence. General Washington ordered Paine's stirring *The American Crisis* read aloud to his disheartened soldiers.

After the war Congress voted Paine $3000, and the state of New York gave him a farm, but he returned to England. Accused of treason there, he fled to France and took part in the French Revolution. He alienated many Americans with his bitter criticism of George Washington, but came back to America in 1802 and settled on his New York farm.

Giambattista Bodoni (1740-1813)

Bodoni, son of a printer, designed the first modern Roman type face. At his press in Parma, under the duke's patronage, he produced elegant and costly books meant to be admired rather than studied—he apparently cared little for editing and proofreading.

Noah Webster (1758-1843)

Webster was born at West Hartford, Connecticut. He fought in the Revolutionary War and then graduated from Yale. An ardent patriot, he devoted his life to standard-

Webster. *United States, 1958.*

izing American grammar and spelling. His "blue-backed speller" was used in every schoolhouse for a hundred years and sold enormous numbers of copies. Webster gave lectures, corresponded with Franklin, wrote political pamphlets, and campaigned for a fair copyright law. He served in the Massachusetts legislature and was one of the founders of Amherst College.

Webster's first dictionary came out in 1806. His *American Dictionary of the English Language* was first published in 1828, and he and his son revised it in 1840. Since then it has been brought up to date many times and has made Webster's name a household word in America.

Robert Burns (1759-1796)

Burns's father was a poor but intelligent Scottish farmer, or "cotter," and young Rob-

Bodoni. *Italy, 1964.*

Burns. *Great Britain, 1966.*

bie loved to read in his father's books of English and Scottish poetry. He wrote his first poems in his teens, while working as a farm laborer. He farmed unsuccessfully with his brother for a few years after his father's death in 1784, and he knew well that farming was a hard way of life. He wrote poems about mirth, poverty, and despair, love songs, drinking songs, and tender poems about the homely country life he lived—"The Cotter's Saturday Night," "To a Mouse," "The Jolly Beggars," and many more.

Burns was handsome and flirtatious. He became engaged in 1786 and arranged to have his poems printed in order to raise money to emigrate with his bride to Jamaica. *Poems, Chiefly in the Scottish Dialect* was a success, and his admirers persuaded him to stay in Scotland. Earnings from the second edition enabled him to travel in the border country, take a farm, and get married. He failed at farming again, but he wrote funny Hallowe'en poems such as "Tam o'Shanter" and touching verses such as "Auld Lang Syne." He drank a lot, and joined a patriotic militia group. At the age of thirty-seven he caught rheumatic fever and died.

Friedrich von Schiller (1759-1805)

Germany's greatest dramatist was the son of an army surgeon. He qualified as a surgeon himself in 1780 but left his regiment without leave to see a performance of his first play, *The Robbers*, which he had published at his own expense. He was arrested and sentenced to publish nothing but medical writings. He fled his native southwestern Germany and wandered over the rest of the country for almost ten years. Unhappy and often ill, he was a leader in the "storm and stress" movement in German literature, a period in which young geniuses rebelled against the literary standards of the past. Schiller wrote ballads and historical studies but he is most famous for his stirring plays, among them *Mary Stuart*, *The Maid of Orleans*, and *William Tell*, which expresses his hatred of tyranny and his love of liberty.

Schiller and Goethe became close friends, and in 1799 Schiller moved to Weimar to be near Goethe and devote the last years of his life to his writing.

Schiller. *Germany–Berlin, 1959.*

Goethe. *Germany, 1961-64.* Goethe's house in Weimar. *German Democratic Republic, 1967.*

Johann Wolfgang von Goethe (1749-1832)

Goethe was born in Frankfurt and spent a happy childhood there. His father was a lawyer, and he reluctantly studied law himself. He managed to forget an unhappy love affair by writing *The Sorrows of Werther*, a sentimental and morbid "storm and stress" novel which was published in 1774 and made him famous overnight. He had also written a successful patriotic play about a robber-knight, *Götz von Berlichingen*.

In 1775 Goethe accepted an invitation from the young Duke of Weimar to reside at his court. Weimar was then the intellectual center of Germany, and Goethe stayed for the rest of his life. He was made a nobleman and served his master well as Chief Minister, but he took little interest in revolutionary politics. He made trips to Italy in 1786-88 and in 1790 and was thrilled and inspired by the purity of classical ideals. He became a leader in the Weimar community—even Napoleon once made a special point of meeting him. Goethe wrote classical plays in verse, two fine novels, an autobiography, and many lyric poems. He began a stimulating correspondence and friendship with the young Schiller. In 1808 Part I of *Faust*, the masterpiece he had begun thirty years earlier, was published after many revisions and much advice from Schiller. Goethe completed Part II just before his death. *Faust* is the story of a disillusioned scholar who seeks happiness in everyday life. He makes a pact with the devil, falls in love with a village girl and is responsible for her death, and is eventually brought to the edge of despair by Mephistopheles.

Goethe was an active and many-sided man who considered his scientific work as important as his literary work. He took part in a geological survey in Weimar, did research in anatomy and discovered a bone in the jaw that was important to the theory of evolution, made studies of leaves and plants, and experimented with optics and colors.

Jakob Grimm (1785-1863) and Wilhelm Grimm (1786-1859)

The Brothers Grimm were German professors and librarians. Their field of study was philology, the science of language, grammar, sounds, and how the families of languages are related to one another. The Grimms made studies of German mythology and edited many old German classics. Jakob wrote a major work on German grammar, and the brothers planned and began a large German dictionary.

They are world-famous for their historic collection of German folk tales known as *Grimm's Fairy Tales.* They walked through the countryside searching out old stories that had been handed down orally from generation to generation, and wrote them all down for the first time. The tales were meant for scholars, and they were rather dull. But then Wilhelm rewrote them using the actual words of the peasant grandmothers, lively and dramatic, and put in plenty of conversation and suspense. The wonderful collection quickly became popular with children and parents everywhere. Some of the best known stories are "Hansel and Gretel," "Cinderella," "Little Red Riding Hood," "Snow White," "The Fisherman and His Wife,""Rumpelstiltskin," "Rapunzel," and "The Wolf and the Seven Little Kids."

The Brothers Grimm. *Germany, 1959.*

Joseph Haydn (1732-1809)

Haydn was born in Austria to simple country parents. As a boy he showed so much musical talent that he was sent to live with a fine but strict teacher. At eight he became one of the famous Vienna choir boys. When he was a young man he became musical director on the estate of Prince Esterházy, one of the many aristocrats of the time who knew and loved good music. These noblemen assured musicians an income, a place to live, and a regular audience for their compositions. Haydn conducted the prince's orchestra and

Scenes from "Snow White and the Seven Dwarfs." *Germany, 1960.*

wrote music for countless concerts and parties. He loved the peaceful countryside and stayed on for thirty years. He was celebrated far and wide but always remained a kindly, religious man who was pleased and proud to have risen so far from his humble beginnings.

He had met Mozart in Vienna, and the older and the younger geniuses became devoted friends. But while Haydn was away in England to conduct and compose for the city of London, Mozart died, leaving his friend in deepest sorrow. Haydn spent his last years alone in Vienna, rich and famous but frail, deaf, and absent-minded. The Viennese adored him, and the Emperor Napoleon personally sent an honor guard to the old gentleman's funeral.

Wolfgang Amadeus Mozart (1756-1791)

Mozart grew up in Salzburg, Austria, where his father was violinist and court musician to the Archbishop. When Wolfgang was only four he so envied his sister's harpsichord lessons and showed such an amazing memory for tunes that his father began teaching him little pieces just for fun. At five Wolfgang composed two little minuets and was already a prodigy on the harpsichord, violin, and organ. When he was six his father took him and his sister on their first concert tour, and

Haydn. *Austria, 1959.*

Mozart. *Austria, 1956.*

Mozart's clavichord. *Germany, 1956.*

Schubert's father was a poor Viennese schoolmaster and amateur cellist who wanted all his children to become teachers. But shy, small Franz was musically gifted, and at eleven he was accepted as a choir boy at the Imperial Chapel. At sixteen he agreed to try teaching, but he hated it and wrote music whenever he could. His only happiness was gathering with his friends to talk and play music. Hardly any of Schubert's work was performed in public until shortly before he died. He sold his lovely songs for very little, and hard work and poverty ruined his health. Although he may never have met Beethoven, Schubert worshipped him and carried a torch in Beethoven's funeral. The following year Schubert died, and his friends arranged to bury him as near as possible to Beethoven. For a long time the manuscripts of his simple, beautiful songs lay in half-forgotten bundles in dusty cupboards in Vienna.

over the next three years the modest, well-mannered lad delighted audiences and stunned professional musicians all over Europe.

As he grew older, however, people did not think he was so wonderful any more, even though in his teens he was already a composer of the rarest daring and brilliance. He settled in Vienna, but never found steady and interesting work. Performances of his compositions were badly reviewed, and Haydn was disgusted with the Viennese for failing to appreciate Mozart's ability. Mozart himself kept his cheerful, hopeful nature in spite of poverty and illness, and managed to write over six hundred works. He began to speak of visits by a mysterious stranger, perhaps Death, and tried desperately to finish a requiem mass. He seemed to have died of a fever, but some people whispered that he had been poisoned by a personal enemy. There was no money for a decent funeral, and Mozart was buried in a pauper's grave.

Schubert. *Austria, 1947.*

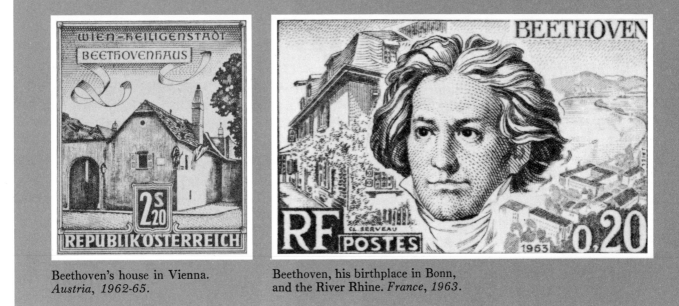

Beethoven's house in Vienna. *Austria, 1962-65.*

Beethoven, his birthplace in Bonn, and the River Rhine. *France, 1963.*

Ludwig van Beethoven (1770-1827)

Beethoven was a native of Bonn, on the Rhine. His father, a singer at the court chapel, often came home drunk, roused his son out of bed in the middle of the night, and forced him to practice the piano in hopes that the boy would become a child prodigy like Mozart. But young Ludwig was stocky, clumsy, and shy, and seldom played with other children. His first kind teacher was the court organist, and his only friend was his gentle, unhappy mother.

At seventeen he visited Vienna and took a few lessons from Mozart, who was greatly impressed with his talent. Called home to his mother's deathbed, he dreamed of going back to study further with Mozart, but Mozart died that same year too. In 1792 Beethoven did

go back to Vienna and studied with Haydn. Haydn thought Beethoven rude and Beethoven found Haydn old-fashioned, but Haydn admitted Beethoven's tremendous ability. When Beethoven performed for members of the nobility he behaved in an arrogant manner, but his music was so superb that a few of the nobles put up with his bad behavior. He dedicated a number of his compositions to these loyal patrons. There was a reason for his irritability: he was worried about his increasing deafness, which eventually ruined his career as a solo pianist. He tried to hide his ailment and, in his despair, refused to see even his closest friends. He never heard his greatest works performed, and during the last ten years of his life he was stone deaf. Still, he insisted on conducting the 1824 premiere of his magnificent *Ninth Symphony*, with its choral setting of Schiller's "Ode to Joy," and he was recognized as the greatest composer of the age.

During a storm in the late winter of 1827 Beethoven lay deathly sick and unconscious. Suddenly there was a thunderclap. He shook his fist at the heavens and died. All Vienna mourned the tragic genius. The schools were closed, and thousands of people wept in the streets as his funeral procession passed by.

Napoleon Bonaparte (1769-1821)

Napoleon was a Corsican of Italian descent. His family was very poor and as a boy he was sickly and hungry. In the French Revolution, with its ideals of liberty, equality, and fraternity, he became a hero and an outstanding military commander. Nicknamed "the little corporal," he possessed great personal charm, and he believed in his own high destiny. As First Consul of France he made peace with the Church, beautified Paris, rooted out corruption in government, and codified French civil law. The Napoleonic Code was adopted by most other European countries.

Beethoven dedicated his "Eroica" Symphony to Napoleon, but soon Napoleon betrayed the glorious ideals of his youth. In 1804 he crowned *himself* Emperor of the French in the presence of the Pope. He overran much of Europe in pursuit of his dream of empire and cared nothing for the welfare of his people. After the English wiped out his fleet at the Battle of Trafalgar, he turned on Russia. He drove his army all the way to Moscow, burned the city, and ordered a retreat, but the endless snows of the Russian winter conquered his once mighty forces. Napoleon had quickly abandoned his army in Russia and assembled a new one in France but he was again defeated. He abdicated and was exiled to the island of Elba. After a year he escaped, mustered his loyal troops, and went into battle at Waterloo, in 1815. Seemingly assured of an easy victory, he suffered a sudden and final defeat, for he was by then ill, fat, and confused. With twenty-four hours to get out of France, he gave himself up to the British and spent his last years on the remote island of St. Helena, brooding over past glory.

Napoleon. *Andorra, 1964.*

THE MIND AND THE SPIRIT

1863-1963 UNITED STATES 5 CENTS

EMANCIPATION PROCLAMATION

IN THE early decades of the American republic many people believed that slavery would gradually die out by itself. George Washington had longed for a plan that would do away with slavery slowly but surely, and in his will he freed his own slaves. Thomas Jefferson worried about the spread of slavery and thought that emancipation followed by deportation might be a workable solution.

In those days the United States had a very small population to inhabit all its vast territory, and during the next generation or two the Deep South enjoyed an economic boom based on sugar and cotton. Many hands were needed to tend the huge plantations upon whose crops prosperity depended, and slaves provided that labor. The new states of Kentucky and Tennessee, with their rich tobacco lands, required farmhands too. So the South stubbornly opposed any talk of abolition. Some slaveowners conscientiously tried to care reasonably well for their slaves, but others treated them with heartless cruelty.

ABOVE: Chain of slavery. *United States, 1963.*

Either way the life of a slave was filled with backbreaking work and was totally without human dignity — a slave, even in the American democracy, was simply not a free man.

The founding fathers, who had written of liberty and justice for all, realized that slavery made no sense in a republic based on the highest ideals. So they hoped and expected that a solution would present itself. Yet the young nation soon entered a period of rapid growth that men like Washington and Jefferson could not possibly have foreseen. The new wealth of the South came from plantation farming and from trading in bustling seaports such as Charleston and New Orleans. The new wealth of the North came from the operations of countless mills and factories that processed the farm products of the South and from the banking services offered in the big cities. Most people were distracted from the horrors and evils of slavery by the fact that slave labor was obviously playing an important part in making the nation richer and more powerful.

The next truly original American leader did not come from the Old South, nor did he appear in the established East. He came out of the new West, from the backwoods on the frontier.

Andrew Jackson (1767-1845)

Jackson was a son of a poor Scotch-Irish immigrant who had cleared a farm in the North Carolina forests. His father died before Andrew was born, and his mother could not even afford a gravestone. She raised her children in humiliating poverty by working as a housekeeper for a relative. Andrew fought in the Revolution as a boy and lost two brothers in the war. Then he studied law and moved westward into Tennessee. A young frontier lawyer was paid mostly in goods, not cash, and Jackson traded in land, horses, and slaves, and began to do well as a cotton planter. He helped draft the state constitution and served as Congressman, Senator, and judge. A veteran Indian fighter, Jackson became a national hero when he commanded a stunning victory over the British at the Battle of New Orleans in 1815.

"Old Hickory," tall and tough, almost won the presidency in 1824, and in 1828 he was swept into office easily. He distrusted Easterners, especially bankers, and they in turn disliked his rough manners and violent temper. Jackson drew his support from the pioneer farmers and shopkeepers west of the Alleghenies, where about a third of the total population already lived, and from the mill-workers of the Eastern towns. Hordes of his backwoods supporters crowded boisterously into the White House at his inauguration, spilling punch on the exquisite furniture and grinding mud into the fine carpets. Their President was honest and fearless, a man of action who governed for the good of the "little man." He served two terms, after which he retired to The Hermitage, an exceptionally handsome brick mansion on his estate near Nashville.

Henry David Thoreau (1817-1862)

Thoreau, son of a pencil maker, was born in Concord, Massachusetts, and was graduated from Harvard. He taught school, gardened, painted houses and built fences, surveyed land, lectured, and wrote for magazines. In his late teens he had begun to devote much of his time to nature study, and kept journals of his observations. In 1845 he built himself a plain cabin in the woods by Walden Pond in Concord and lived there alone for over two years. In *Walden, or Life in the Woods*, published in 1854, Thoreau described how he built the simple house, watched the animals of the woodland, grew beans and potatoes for his meals and made occasional trips to the village for supplies. He wrote of his belief in the dignity of man and of the values that made life worthwhile for him. He was an individualist who deliberately withdrew from conventional civilization and proved that he could provide for his own personal and spiritual needs.

Thoreau spent a short time in jail in 1848 for refusing to pay his poll taxes to support the Mexican War, which he contended was an unjust war. It was there that he wrote his provocative pamphlet "Civil Disobedience."

Jackson. *United States, 1967.*   Thoreau. *United States, 1967.*

Lincoln. *United States, 1959.*

Abraham Lincoln (1809-1865)

Abe Lincoln was born in a log cabin in Kentucky. He lost his mother when he was nine, and picked up what education he had by himself. He worked on the farm, split fence rails, kept a store, and began the practice of law in Springfield, Illinois. Six feet four inches tall, gaunt, and black-haired, he served eight years in the Illinois legislature and one term in Congress. He ran for the Senate and did not win, but he attracted nationwide attention and in 1860 was elected President.

By his inauguration in March, 1861, six southern states had already left the Union. Lincoln considered slavery a moral, social, and political evil, but he did not plan its immediate abolition. During the Civil War he held immense power but he trusted in the intelligence of the people and guided the nation wisely. Always a natural politician, he grew to be a great and patient statesman. He hoped the secessionist states would return to the Union, and he took pains not to offend the border states. Honest and realistic, he hesitated to free the slaves until 1863, when on January 1 he issued the formal Emancipation Proclamation, freeing the slaves in the rebel states but not elsewhere in the Union. He meant to end the war quickly by reducing the South's manpower and adding to the Union's prestige overseas. The decision tormented him, but he concluded that "these rebels are violating the Constitution to destroy the Union: I will violate the Constitution, if necessary, to save the Union."

Lincoln pledged the South an honorable and generous peace, but the war dragged on. At last, after several decisive Union victories, Lee surrendered on April 9, 1865. Only five days later, while attending the theater in Washington, Lincoln was mortally wounded by an assassin's bullet. His funeral train traveled slowly over the seventeen hundred miles back to Springfield. His simple epitaph reads: "Now he belongs to the ages."

Dostoevsky. *Bulgaria, 1957.*

Tolstoy. *Czechoslovakia, 1953.*

Feodor Dostoevsky (1821-1881)

This Russian novelist, son of a surgeon, was born in Moscow. He graduated from military college but turned immediately to writing. In 1849, condemned for his part in a plot against the tsar, he went before a firing squad. At the last minute he was sentenced instead to hard labor in Siberia. There he suffered from epileptic attacks and turned more and more to religion. After ten years he returned, and edited magazines in St. Petersburg. He could not resist gambling, and repeatedly lost all his money. Dostoevsky was preoccupied with the problem of guilt. He felt pity for all men, and believed that even the worst sinner was capable of redemption. His gripping, realistic novels *Crime and Punishment* and *The Brothers Karamazov* are peopled with unforgettable and complex characters.

Leo Tolstoy (1828-1910)

Count Leo Tolstoy's family lived on an estate in Russia. As a typical young nobleman he served in the army, and then he retired to his estate to write and study. His first tales and sketches dealt with the horrors of war. He mastered the psychological novel with *Anna Karenina*, and worked for six years on *War and Peace*, a saga of two families and a Russian epic of defeat, struggle, and eventual victory over Napoleon.

In middle age Tolstoy experienced a spiritual conversion to a new Christianity based on non-violence and a simple way of life. He gave his wife his land and fortune and lived as poorly as a peasant. One night, after a quarrel with her, he left his house secretly. He caught a chill and died in a railroad station in the company of one of his daughters, still refusing to see his wife.

Dickens. *Russia, 1962.*

Whitman. *Czechoslovakia, 1955.*

Charles Dickens (1812-1870)

Dickens spent a miserable childhood in London. As a boy he had to go to work in a warehouse when his father was put into debtor's prison. He gained his "education" mainly from reading and wandering through the filthy, crowded streets. In his teens he was a lawyer's apprentice and court reporter. To support his wife and their ten children he turned out novel after novel in sentimental and suspenseful monthly installments for magazines. He created memorable characters against colorful and sometimes squalid backgrounds and was the most popular English novelist of his time. He was often near collapse from overwork. Among his many novels, some of which hastened much-needed social reforms, are *Oliver Twist*, *David Copperfield* (partly autobiographical), and *Great Expectations*.

Walt Whitman (1819-1892)

"The good gray poet" of democracy, a Quaker, was born on Long Island and moved to Brooklyn, New York, at the age of four. He worked as an office boy, country schoolteacher, typesetter, reporter, and editor of several newspapers in Brooklyn and New Orleans.

In 1855 he published a volume of poems, *Leaves of Grass*, in which he tried to embody all of modern man and modern life. The poems were called daring and indecent and were widely criticized, but over the years the book grew to almost four hundred pages in revised editions. During the Civil War Whitman served as a volunteer nurse in Union army hospitals, and he wrote stirring poems in memory of President Lincoln. He was partially paralyzed in 1873 and was supported by a few admirers.

Charles Darwin (1809-1882)

Darwin's father was a physician and his grandfather was a pioneer physiologist. He studied medicine, then started studying for the ministry, and instead became deeply interested in geology and botany. He sailed as official naturalist on the five year voyage of HMS *Beagle* (1831-35) around South America and the South Pacific, gathering information on plants, animals, and land formations of the coasts and islands. On the desolate but enchanting Galapagos Islands Darwin noted that the turtles and finches of each island were not exactly alike. He concluded that species can change and develop new characteristics as a result of their environment.

A kind and affectionate man, Darwin lived on a private income on his estate in Kent and performed experiments in his gardens and conservatories. He worked out a theory of evolution, published in 1859 as *On the Origin of the Species by Means of Natural Selection*. In 1871 he published *The Descent of Man*, in which he traced the human race, as well as gorillas, chimpanzees, and orangutans, all back to a group of common ancestors. Darwin was not the first to propose a theory of evolution, but he was the first to convince most of his fellow biologists of the basic validity of such a theory.

Louis Pasteur (1822-1895)

Pasteur came from the Jura region of France. He became professor of chemistry at the Sorbonne in Paris in 1867. With his discovery of the bacilli that caused two silkworm diseases he was able to save the French silk industry. Pasteur proved that the fermentation of milk, wine and beer is caused by tiny organisms, and found a method of preventing harmful growths in beer. His process known as "pasteurization" is a way of treat-

Darwin. *Poland, 1959.* Pasteur. *Poland, 1959.*

Mendel. *Czechoslovakia, 1965.* Koch. *Germany–Berlin, 1960.*

ing liquids to make them safe for human consumption—the food is kept at 145 degrees for thirty minutes and then is quickly cooled.

Pasteur also learned how to control chicken cholera, showed that sheep and cows could be vaccinated against severe attacks of anthrax, and developed a cure and a preventive treatment for rabies in dogs and hydrophobia in humans. He used it successfully in 1885 on a child that had been bitten by a mad dog.

Gregor Johann Mendel (1822-1884)

Mendel, a peasant's son, was a native of Austrian Silesia. He was ordained a priest, studied science in Vienna for two years, and returned to his native province to teach science at Brünn. He became abbot of the Augustinian cloister there in 1868. Mendel performed his botanical experiments mainly with garden peas, cross-breeding the plants systematically. He was the first to keep careful records for several "generations" of plants. His research enabled him to formulate his laws of dominant and recessive characteristics. Mendel's conclusions were published by a local natural history society but his work

was overlooked during his lifetime. His poor eyesight and his duties at the cloister limited his activities too. Yet his experiments in the monastery garden form the basis for modern genetics, the study of heredity, and the breeding of improved strains of plants and animals.

Robert Koch (1843-1910)

Koch, born in the Harz Mountain region of Germany, was a practicing physician. About 1872 he began to do research on wounds and septicemia. He led a German expedition to Egypt and India to study cholera, and later became a professor at the University in Berlin and director of the Institute for Infectious Diseases. Koch discovered many organisms that cause contagious diseases in animals and human beings, including anthrax, tuberculosis, and cholera. In 1890 he produced tuberculin, which is used in the diagnosis of tuberculosis. After studying cattle plague in South Africa he developed a vaccine against it, and he investigated bubonic plague in India and malaria and sleeping sickness in Africa. In 1905 Koch received the Nobel Prize in Physiology and Medicine.

Morse. *United States, 1940.*

Edison. *United States, 1947.*

Samuel F. B. Morse (1791-1872)

The eldest son of a Massachusetts clergyman-geographer, Morse went to Yale and then studied painting in England. He became a well-known portrait painter after his return to the United States in 1815, and helped found the National Academy of Design. Morse was also interested in chemistry and electricity, however, and in 1832 he managed to transmit messages using electric current and a little machine he had invented. People laughed at his claims when he showed his invention to Congress, and he was unable to patent it in Europe. After twelve years Congress finally appropriated him $30,000 to string the world's first telegraph wires between Washington and Baltimore. On May 24, 1844, Morse sent the first long-distance message: "What hath God wrought!" He later invented Morse code and organized the Western Union Company. In 1866 a permanent cable was laid underwater all the way from Newfoundland to Ireland.

Thomas Alva Edison (1847-1931)

Edison's parents were Dutch immigrants to Canada, then the United States. He grew up in Michigan. Alva quit school early and went to work as a newsboy on a railway line that ran into Detroit, and after buying some old printing type he published the first newspaper ever printed on a train. One day he saved the life of the stationmaster's child, and as a reward he received some lessons in operating the telegraph. He worked as an operator in several American and Canadian towns but disliked the routine work.

In 1870 he sold the rights to some of his patents for $40,000 and set up a workshop. In 1879 he settled in Menlo Park, New Jersey, and that same year he perfected the incandescent light bulb. The "wizard of Menlo Park" went on to invent a vote recorder, a telegraph system for sending messages to moving trains, a mimeograph machine, the phonograph, and motion pictures. All in all he held over a thousand patents, and he re-

Mergenthaler. *Germany–Berlin, 1954.*

ceived a gold medal from Congress for his services to mankind.

Ottmar Mergenthaler (1854-1899)

As a boy Mergenthaler, son of a German village schoolteacher, repaired a broken church clock that had puzzled all the experts. He was apprenticed to a watchmaker, and at eighteen he emigrated to the United States. He inspected and fixed clocks in government buildings in Washington and worked for his cousin, building models for inventors. He soon grew so much involved with plans of his own that he set up a workshop in Baltimore. There he perfected the linotype, a machine operated by means of a keyboard, which made metal slugs to take the place of lines of handset type. He patented it in 1844, and it was first used at the New York *Herald Tribune* in 1886.

Alexander Graham Bell (1847-1922)

Bell was born in Edinburgh, Scotland. His father was a teacher of the deaf, and Bell carried on his father's work. He moved to Canada and then to the United States. In 1865 he had the idea of transmitting speech by means of electric waves. He worked in Boston, teaching deaf-mutes, from the year 1871, and by 1875 had developed his revolutionary invention, the telephone. He patented it in 1876 and the following year organized the Bell Telephone Company. The telephone was an immediate success and made Bell wealthy and famous. Bell also invented an improved recorder for Edison's phonograph and established the Volta Laboratory, which produced the first successful phonograph record. With other scientists he worked at investigating the problem of stability and balance in flying machines.

Bell. *Canada, 1947.*

POSTE ITALIANE L.15

GIUSEPPE
GARIBALDI
1807 1882

DEUTSCHE BUNDESPOST

20

1815 OTTO VON BISMARCK 1898

Garibaldi. *Italy, 1957.*   Bismarck. *Germany, 1965.*

Giuseppe Garibaldi (1807-1882)

The popular hero of Italy's struggle for national unification served in the navy as a young man. He was sentenced to death for taking part in an unsuccessful republican plot, but fled to South America. After his return over ten years later, he fought with the Sardinian army against Austria, master of much of Italy. Austria won, and Garibaldi fled this time to the United States. He lived for several years in New York City and became an American citizen. By the time he went back to Italy in 1854 he had given up his dream of an Italian republic.

In May of 1860 Garibaldi led an expedition of a thousand volunteer "Red Shirts" in a dramatic invasion of Sicily and Naples. The people cheered him as their new ruler but he turned over the territory to King Victor Emmanuel of Sardinia as he had promised he would. He then retired to his peaceful island farm.

Otto von Bismarck (1815-1898)

Bismarck was a member of the privileged landed aristocracy of Prussia, a social class opposed to the liberal ideals of the 1848 revolutionaries who had hoped in vain to set up a constitutional democracy in Germany. Bismarck favored a union of the many small German states under Prussia and resented Austria's leading role in German affairs. He served in the legislature, as ambassador to France and Russia, and was appointed premier in 1862. With the king's full approval he strengthened the Prussian army, stirred up a wave of patriotism by reviving an old border dispute with Denmark, and picked a quarrel with Austria. Always a man of dizzyingly fast action, he then formed a North German Confederation and convinced Austria's South German allies to join it. Continuing his policy of "blood and iron" Bismarck deliberately provoked a war with France and quickly won. In 1871, at the Palace of Versailles outside Paris, the German Empire was proclaimed, with Prince Bismarck as its first chancellor.

The "iron chancellor" formed convenient security alliances and brought about many social and economic reforms. In spite of his tight reorganization of German life he was the most popular man in the nation. In 1888, however, Kaiser Wilhelm II came to the throne. After a two-year power struggle with the new emperor, Bismarck was dismissed and retired to his estate.

Richard Wagner (1813-1883)

Wagner was raised in the lovely German city of Dresden. His first opera was a success, but several others were slow to win any notice. Still, he considered himself the greatest musician who ever lived and a great poet as well. He developed a radical new theory of "music drama" that would combine all the arts. Conservative Germany did not seem to appreciate his genius, however, and he lived abroad for years. Obsessed with his own importance, Wagner lived beyond his means on loans he never meant to repay, "used" his friends mercilessly for his own advantage, and tolerated no criticism.

He first published his life's work, *The Ring of the Nibelungs*, a cycle of four dramas based on Germanic myths, as a poem. Then, in 1864, the eccentric King Ludwig II of Bavaria invited him to Munich and commissioned him to finish the musical score for *The Ring*. Afterwards Wagner was able to design his own festival theater in the town of Bayreuth to accommodate the huge orchestra his scores demanded. In 1876 the theater opened with the historic first performance of the complete *Ring*, so vast and difficult that Wagner himself had never expected it could actually be staged.

Wagner died in Venice. He is buried in the garden of his villa in Bayreuth.

Opening bars of Wagner's opera "Die Meistersinger." *Germany, 1968.*

Wagner and "The Flying Dutchman." *German Democratic Republic, 1963.*

Henrik Ibsen (1828-1906)

The Norwegian playwright Ibsen originally began the study of medicine. When his father lost his money in business speculations Ibsen, then sixteen, went to work as a chemist's assistant. He wrote a play but it was rejected, and he worked for several years as a journalist. In 1851 he became stage director and playwright at the National Theater in Bergen and was later associated with theaters in Oslo and Copenhagen.

For twenty-eight years Ibsen lived abroad, mostly in Italy and Germany, because he disagreed with political developments in Norway. He wrote a series of controversial realistic dramas during those years, including *A Doll's House*, *Ghosts*, *The Master Builder*, *An Enemy of the People*, and *Hedda Gabler*, which show courageous individuals rebelling against the empty social customs of the time. Ibsen is also famous for his fine dramatic poem *Peer Gynt*.

Anton Pavlovich Chekhov (1860-1904)

Chekhov, son of a poor Russian shopkeeper and grandson of a serf, was a physician, but he seldom practiced medicine. As a student he had written many humorous pieces for magazines. His early short stories were quite well received, but several plays were failures. An excellent revival of his play *The Seagull* at the renowned Moscow Art Theater encouraged him, and he went on to write *Uncle Vanya*, *The Three Sisters*, and *The Cherry Orchard*, all of which were successful.

Chekhov was deeply concerned over the dullness and emptiness of middle-class life and the loneliness of individuals. He believed that work was the only solution for people who were struggling to escape the hopelessness they felt because of the lack of purpose and satisfaction in their daily lives. Because of poor health Chekhov spent more and more time outside Russia. He died of tuberculosis in Germany at the age of forty-four.

Ibsen. *Bulgaria, 1957.*   Chekhov. *Czechoslovakia, 1954.*

Eleanora Duse. *Italy, 1958.*   Sarah Bernhardt. *France, 1945.*

Eleanora Duse (1859-1924)

The Italian actress Duse was born near Venice to a theatrical family. She began her career in traveling acting companies and made her debut at fourteen as Shakespeare's Juliet. She appeared in Naples and Milan and in her twenties had already established a glowing reputation. She toured all over Europe and made her American debut in 1893. Duse's acting style was extremely simple but powerful and highly emotional. She avoided exaggerated effects. For many years she and Sarah Bernhardt were great rivals. Both actresses drew huge crowds who argued hotly in favor of one or the other. Duse enjoyed the final triumph when the Paris critics declared her the better actress. She was particularly noted for her interpretations of leading roles in Ibsen's plays.

Eleanora Duse gave up acting in 1909 but made a motion picture in 1916 and returned to the stage after all in 1921.

Sarah Bernhardt (1844-1923)

Sarah Bernhardt's real name was Rosine Bernard. Her parents were French Roman Catholics of Jewish descent and she was raised in a convent. Her acting debut, at seventeen, was not a success, but soon she was touring the continent, Britain, and the United States, performing in French at the most illustrious theaters of the world. She was a legendary personality who indulged in outlandish publicity stunts—she once made a dangerous ascent in a balloon, and she kept wild animals as pets in her mansion. It was rumored that she slept in a coffin instead of a bed. She was a versatile actress but primarily a tragedienne. Her voice was strong and resonant, and she gestured in the grand manner. "The divine Sarah" owned and managed the Théatre Sarah Bernhardt in Paris. She appeared in two silent films in 1912. Her leg had to be amputated in 1915 but she continued her stage career in spite of her disability.

Selma Lagerlof. *Sweden, 1958.*

Andersen. *Czechoslovakia, 1955.*

Selma Lagerlöf (1858-1940)

The author of *The Wonderful Adventures of Nils* came from the province of Värmland in Sweden. For ten years she worked as a teacher in a girls' school, and wrote many popular tales, some novels, and an autobiography.

In 1902 the government of Sweden asked her to write a book that would teach Swedish children the geography of their land. *Nils,* published in 1906, was the book, a long but delightful story of a mean, rough country boy who finds himself magically reduced to the size of an elf. He flies away on the back of a gander with a flock of wild geese that migrates all over the country. Nils learns about the history of Sweden, the people, folklore, and wild life. He also learns to be considerate and loyal to his friends. Selma Lagerlöf won the Nobel Prize for Literature in 1909.

Hans Christian Andersen (1805-1875)

Scandinavia's beloved storyteller was born in the Danish town of Odense. His father, a poor shoemaker, died when his son was little, and the boy's childhood was a sad and impoverished time. Although he showed talent for writing poetry, he had to go to work in a factory. At fourteen he went to Copenhagen to seek his fortune. He tried acting but had no luck because he did not have enough education, and he was just as unsuccessful as a singer. Through the help of some generous friends he applied to the king, who sent him to school for several years. Andersen was unhappy there but he passed his examinations and received a travel grant from the king. He wrote sketches of life in Germany, Switzerland, and Italy, and tried writing poems and fantasies.

A novel was a success in 1835, and the same year Andersen's first volume of fairy tales, *Eventyr*, appeared. At last he had discovered his special gift, and he eventually published as many as one new volume of tales a year. Among his best-loved stories are "The Emperor's New Clothes," "The Little Mermaid," "The Ugly Duckling," and "The Snow Queen."

Mark Twain (1835-1910)

Samuel Langhorne Clemens spent his childhood in Hannibal, Missouri, on the Mississippi River. His father died when Sam was twelve, and the boy worked for a few years on his brother's newspaper in Hannibal and as a printer in the East. In 1857 he went to New Orleans on his way to make his fortune in South America, but became a river pilot instead. When the Civil War closed the Mississippi traffic, he went to Nevada. He had no luck in get-rich-quick schemes but wrote for a newspaper there under the byline "Mark Twain," the pen name he took from the river pilot's cry meaning "two fathoms sounded."

Twain published his first big success in 1865 as a reporter in San Francisco: a short story called "The Celebrated Jumping Frog of Calaveras County." It made him famous, and he enjoyed considerable success as a humorous lecturer. He eventually settled in Connecticut, where he wrote his three classics *The Adventures of Tom Sawyer*, *Life on the Mississippi*, and *The Adventures of Huckleberry Finn*, incomparable recollections of his river-town boyhood and his steamboating days in the heart of America. In 1893 the publishing company of which he was a partner went out of business and plunged him into debt. He tried without success to manufacture typesetting machines and then set out on a wearying lecture tour around the world to pay back what he owed. He published amusing travel books and many articles. Twain's last years were filled with sorrow—he lost two of his daughters and his beloved wife, who had been ill for a long time.

Mark Twain. *Russia, 1960.*

Louis Braille (1809-1852)

Louis Braille was born near Paris. He was blinded in an accident when he was three, and at the age of ten he entered the Institution des Jeunes Aveugles, a school for blind children in Paris. He stayed on there as a teacher. Braille was devoted to the study of music and played the organ well. The system of raised printing he invented is universally used to print both reading material and musical scores for the blind. It consists of sixty-three different combinations of six dots.

Florence Nightingale (1820-1910)

This famous nurse was born in Florence, Italy, to wealthy English parents, and trained in her profession in France and Germany. At thirty-three she became superintendent of a women's hospital in London. After war broke out between England and Russia, Florence Nightingale defied much opposition to organize a group of thirty-eight nurses who left for the Crimea to care for the wounded. The nurses arrived at the front in November of 1854, just in time to receive the casualties of a bloody battle. Soon there were ten thousand soldiers under the care of "the lady of the lamp" and her staff. Nurse Nightingale was shocked at the poor sanitation and overcrowded conditions in the field hospitals, and she worked tirelessly to improve the situation. The death rate from dysentery, cholera, and typhus dropped sharply.

Florence Nightingale returned to England in 1856. She used a testimonial subscription fund of fifty thousand pounds to found a nurses' training school and home in London. Her own health was broken, but she spent many more years of her long life advising on sanitation reform in military hospitals and the improvement of public health in India. She was the first woman ever to receive the British Order of Merit, awarded to her in 1907.

Braille. *France, 1948.*   Florence Nightingale. *Belgium, 1939.*

Wilhelm Konrad von Roentgen (1845-1923)

The Prussian physicist Roentgen studied at Zürich, Switzerland, and was a professor at several German universities. In 1895, while he was teaching at Würzburg, he discovered invisible electro-magnetic rays of short-wave length, which he called "X-rays." He did important research also on the heat-conducting properties of crystals and the specific heat of gases. He was the recipient of the first Nobel Prize for Physics, in 1901, for his discovery of the X-ray.

Marie Curie (1867-1934)

Maria Sklodowska was a native of Warsaw, Poland, and studied with her father, a physics teacher. In 1891 she went to Paris to study at the Sorbonne, and received her doctorate in 1904. She married a professor of physics there, Pierre Curie, and worked with him on problems in magnetism and radioactivity. They shared the 1903 Nobel Prize in Physics with a third scientist. The Curies studied uranium, a radioactive element in pitchblende, and discovered two new elements, polonium and radium. They refused to patent the process by which they isolated radium and thus took no profits from commercial uses of their methods. Pierre Curie was killed in a traffic accident in Paris in 1906, and his wife succeeded him as a Sorbonne professor.

Madame Curie won a second Nobel Prize, this time in Chemistry, in 1911—she was the first person ever to win two Nobel Prizes. During World War I she organized radiological services in hospitals, and in 1919 she was made an honorary professor of radiology at the University of Warsaw. She had two daughters, one a chemist who won a Nobel Prize in 1935, and the other a musician and writer.

Roentgen. *Spain, 1967.*

Madame Curie. *France, 1967.*

STRUGGLE FOR PEACE

Das Lied vom Sturmvogel
MAXIM GORKI

THE Russian playwright Chekhov, along with many other late-19th-Century writers, sensed that something was wrong with contemporary life. He wrote over and over about the loneliness people had to endure as they lived out their aimless days. Scientists were challenging long-accepted "truths" such as the Creation of earth and man, and searching for the keys to life and death. For the first time in years people realized that it was their responsibility to act, to try to relieve some of the man-made misery and poverty all around them.

From Germany, land of many original thinkers, came a radical theory about the immense problems of the new industrial society. Then, in Russia, whose writers had so vividly portrayed the inner sorrows of the human soul, came the revolution. It swept away forever the old traditions, whether good or bad, and led to a new way of government that demanded the full allegiance of the masses—a kind of loyalty commanded in earlier centuries only by the Church.

ABOVE: Stormy petrel and toppling towers. *German Democratic Republic, 1968.*

Karl Marx (1818-1883)

Marx was born in Trier, Germany, descendant of a long line of rabbis. In 1848, with his associate Friedrich Engels, he published "The Communist Manifesto" and had to flee the police because of his radical ideas. He spent the rest of his life in London. Often sick, he supported his family on money from Engels and fees for his newspaper articles.

No one paid much attention to Marx until he founded the International Workingmen's Association in 1864. The first volume of his masterwork *Das Kapital (Capital)* was published in 1867, and it was so tedious that even the strict tsars allowed it to be published in Russia—they were sure no one would understand it. Marx regarded history as one long struggle between the rich and the poor. The rich grew richer and the poor grew poorer because the capitalists, who owned the tools the workers used, spent their profits to buy more tools, which the workers then used to produce still more profits for the capitalists. Marx called upon the workers of the world to unite and fight for a share of the wealth. As Marx saw it, the capitalist system had brought about the existence of a working class and was exploiting the workers. He believed the workingmen's lot would get worse and worse until they rebelled and destroyed the unjust system.

Nikolai Lenin (1870-1924)

When Lenin was a young man his brother was executed for taking part in a plot to kill the tsar. He gave up his law practice to study the works of Karl Marx and was sent to Siberia for organizing an illegal "union for the liberation of the working class." In exile in Switzerland in 1900 Lenin organized a Marxist party to prepare for the revolution. After a revolution in 1905 was crushed, he spent the next twelve years in underground activities as leader of the Bolsheviks, or extreme branch of Marxists. Then, in 1917, the tsar was deposed. Lenin hurried from Switzerland to Russia in a sealed train, crossing wartime Germany by special permission. In October the moderate provisional government in Russia collapsed. In 1918 Lenin became premier and ruthlessly established a "dictatorship of the proletariat." The tsar and his family were shot. Karl Marx had never called for terrorism, but Lenin, shrewd, cold, and single-minded, was revered almost as a god by the people of Soviet Russia after his death. His body lies in a crystal coffin in Red Square in Moscow.

Marx. *Russia, 1968.*

Lenin. *Russia, 1968.*

Ford and 1909 Model T. *United States, 1968.*

Daimler car of 1886. *Germany, 1961.*

Henry Ford (1863-1947)

Ford grew up on a farm near Dearborn, Michigan. At sixteen he went to work as an apprentice machinist. He made $2.50 a week and added another couple of dollars to his weekly income on a second job as a watch repairman. In 1893 he built himself the first gasoline-driven motor car, which made lots of noise, scared horses, and blocked traffic. It attracted crowds of curious people who often could not resist trying to run the car themselves, so Ford had to chain it to a lamppost whenever he parked it.

The Ford Motor Company, founded in 1903, gave America an inexpensive vehicle, mass produced on the assembly line from standard parts. The horse-and-buggy days were over! The 1908 Ford Model T cost over $800, but before long the assembly lines at Ford were turning out an improved Model T for as little as $310. Ford was a capitalist who did care about his workers, and in 1914 he startled other businessmen by voluntarily setting a minimum daily wage of $5.00, about twice what most industrial workers got. Ford employees were among the first to work a five-day week, and they participated in one of the first profit-sharing plans.

In 1936 Henry Ford and his son set up the Ford Foundation, the world's largest private trust fund. It aids education, culture, scientific research, and furthers the cause of peace and democracy. Ford used more of his immense fortune to build Greenfield Village at Dearborn. He put up the houses and workshops of many great Americans—actual buildings, furnishings, and even trees. Noah Webster's house is there and so is Edison's Menlo Park laboratory.

Wilbur Wright (1867-1912) and Orville Wright (1871-1948)

The Wright brothers, American pioneers in the field of aviation, became interested in flying in the mid-1890's. They made their first experiments with kites and gliders that they built in their bicycle repair shop in Dayton, Ohio. They improved the glider and Orville designed an engine for it. They became the first men to fly in a heavier-than-air flying machine when they successfully tested a plane on the beach at Kitty Hawk, North Carolina, on December 17, 1903. It stayed in the air twelve seconds and traveled one hundred twenty feet.

The Wrights continued their experiments and in 1905 they made a successful circular flight of twenty-four and a half miles, lasting over thirty-three minutes, at Dayton. The next year they received a patent on a flying machine, and in 1908 they went to France to make exhibition flights. They completed a plane for the United States War Department but it crashed—they managed to repair it and

The Wright Brothers. *United States, 1949.*

tested it with success in 1909. After abandoning their bicycle business they founded a company to manufacture airplanes under their own patent. Wilbur Wright was president of the company until his death, but three years later Orville sold it to devote all his time to research.

Amelia Earhart (1898-1937)

Amelia Earhart was born in Atchison, Kansas. She was a teacher and social worker in Massachusetts. In June of 1928 she became the first woman to fly across the Atlantic as a passenger, from Newfoundland to Wales. From 1928 to 1930 she worked as aviation editor for a magazine. Then, in 1932, she flew the Atlantic to Ireland by herself, and in 1935 flew "solo" from Honolulu, Hawaii, to California. She was the first woman ever to make both flights unaccompanied. In July of 1937, during an attempt to fly around the world, Amelia Earhart's plane mysteriously disappeared between New Guinea and Howland Island in the South Pacific, and she and her radio operator were never heard from again. Her autobiography, *Last Flight*, was edited and published by her husband after her death.

Amelia Earhart. *United States, 1963.*

□ □

Fridtjof Nansen (1861-1930)

When the Norwegian Nansen was twenty-one he sailed away to the Arctic in the sealer *Viking*. On his return he became keeper of the natural history department at the Bergen museum. He made an adventurous trip from east to west across the ice fields of Greenland. During the years 1893-96 Nansen partially achieved his exciting goal of reaching the North Pole by allowing the round-hulled polar ship *Fram* to be frozen into the ice north of Siberia and then letting it drift with the current over the Pole towards Greenland. He reached the highest latitude then attained by man, 86° 14′ N. Even though he did not reach the Pole he gathered a great deal of valuable information. Nansen then became a professor of zoology and oceanography at Oslo and wrote several books. He directed the International Commission for Study of the Sea and made several new scientific voyages, mainly in the North Atlantic.

He worked for the political separation of Norway from Sweden, which took place in 1905, and served as independent Norway's first minister to Great Britain. This statesman-scientist was honored all over the world for his humanitarian activities. After the First World War he helped send refugees and war prisoners back to their homes, and he directed Red Cross famine relief in Russia in the early 1920's. He represented his native land on the League of Nations Disarmament Commission, and was awarded the Nobel Peace Prize in 1922.

Roald Amundsen (1872-1928)

Amundsen was born in Borge, Norway. He began studying medicine but soon gave it up for a life at sea. In 1897 he served as first mate of the Belgian ship *Belgica* on an expedition to the Antarctic. He was commander of the smack *Gjöa*, which undertook the first navigation of the Northwest Passage during 1903-06, and during this voyage he fixed the position of the North Magnetic Pole. He completed the passage in 1920.

In December of 1911 Amundsen became the first man ever to reach the South Pole, one month ahead of the famous explorer Scott. The Amundsen expedition sailed in the same

Amundsen. *Norway, 1961.*

Nansen. *Norway, 1961.*

Schweitzer. *Monaco, 1955.*

Schweitzer's hospital at Lambarene. *Monaco, 1955.*

specially built polar ship *Fram* that Nansen had used. In 1926 Amundsen flew over the North Pole from Spitsbergen to Alaska. Two years later Amundsen's plane disappeared over the ocean. He had been trying to rescue a former comrade who had been lost returning from the Pole.

Albert Schweitzer (1875-1965)

Albert Schweitzer was raised in the French-German province of Alsace. He attended school near home, and later studied the organ, philosophy, and theology in Strasbourg, Paris, and Berlin. At twenty-one he resolved that he would live for science and music until he reached the age of thirty, and then devote the rest of his life to the service of humanity. He published a study of Bach and an essay on the design of the organ. In 1905, true to his vow, he entered medical school.

Schweitzer married in 1913 and started out with his bride for Lambaréné, a deserted mission station in French Equatorial Africa (now Gabon). Schweitzer, a devout Protestant, often spoke of "reverence for life," and the hospital he founded in the jungle reflected his Christian faith. He spent the rest of his life—over fifty years—in Africa except for occasional trips to Europe to raise money by giving organ recitals. In 1952 Schweitzer won the Nobel Peace Prize. His daughter, who administered the hospital for many years, has continued to run it since her father's death at ninety.

Pirandello. *Italy, 1967.*

Luigi Pirandello (1867-1936)

Pirandello, a native of Sicily, was a lecturer in literature in Rome for twenty-five years. He was the author of some three hundred short stories, six novels, and about fifty plays. He is best known for his fascinating, ultramodern dramas, filled with wit and intellect. Pirandello's characters are not fixed and definite personalities—they seem different to different people, and audiences react differently to them. Viewers of Pirandello plays ask themselves which is the *real* reality (or is there any such thing?). In 1925 Pirandello established his own theater in Rome and took his plays on tour in Europe. His best known dramas are *Six Characters in Search of an Author* and *Right You Are If You Think So.* Films have been made of several of his works. In 1934 Pirandello won the Nobel Prize for Literature.

George Bernard Shaw (1856-1950)

Shaw was born in Dublin, Ireland, but at twenty he left for London, where his mother had found work as a singing teacher and his sister was a musical comedy actress. Five novels of his were turned down by publishers. He worked as music and drama critic for several newspapers and was enthusiastic about Wagner and Ibsen. He also wrote many essays in favor of Socialism. In 1898 his *Plays Pleasant and Unpleasant* appeared, and by 1932 his complete works filled thirty volumes. He was awarded the Nobel Prize in Literature for the year 1925. All Shaw's writings are crisp and clever, and his women characters are especially charming. Among his most popular plays are *Man and Superman, Heartbreak House, Saint Joan,* and *Pygmalion* (on which the musical *My Fair Lady* was based). Movie versions of his plays have been very popular.

Shaw was a vegetarian who did not drink and disliked tobacco. He lived to be ninety-four, and his sharp wit and fantastic energy delighted his admirers.

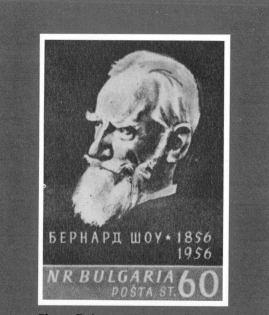

Shaw. *Bulgaria, 1957.*

O'Neill. *United States, 1967.*

Wright. *United States, 1965.*

Eugene O'Neill (1888-1953)

O'Neill, born in New York City, spent his childhood in New London, Connecticut. His father was an actor. Eugene attended college briefly and then worked as a seaman and newspaperman. In 1915 he joined the Provincetown Players, and wrote several short plays. His first Broadway play, in 1920, won him a Pulitzer Prize. O'Neill wrote only one comedy, and his long, brooding dramas explore conflicts among individuals. He was haunted all his life by his own troubled relationship with his parents. Among his finest plays of the American scene are *Strange Interlude*, *Long Day's Journey into Night*, and *The Iceman Cometh*. He revised his plays many times and worked on them for years.

The winner of four Pulitzer Prizes in all, O'Neill became the first American dramatist to win the Nobel Prize for Literature in 1936. During the last decade of his life he was so sick at times that he could not hold a pencil. He spent his last years going over his plays and trying to make sure that they would survive in the exact versions he intended.

Frank Lloyd Wright (1869-1959)

Wright, a native of Wisconsin, first studied civil engineering. When the new wing of a university building suddenly collapsed, he decided to try to apply the principles of engineering to architecture. In and around Chicago he designed a striking series of low, modern houses with projecting eaves in "prairie style," planned to conform with the local landscape. A daring and controversial architect, Wright used native stone, textured wood, and prefabricated materials. The walls and roofs of his houses enclosed the more important spaces within. All his designs—homes, hotels, public buildings—combine beauty with efficiency and comfort.

Wright founded a cultural experiment in the arts, the Taliesin Fellowship, on his Wisconsin estate, and a workshop in Arizona called Taliesin West. His first building in New York City was the Solomon R. Guggenheim Museum, a continuous concrete spiral with a dizzying ramp in the interior. It was finished only a few months after Wright's death, in 1959.

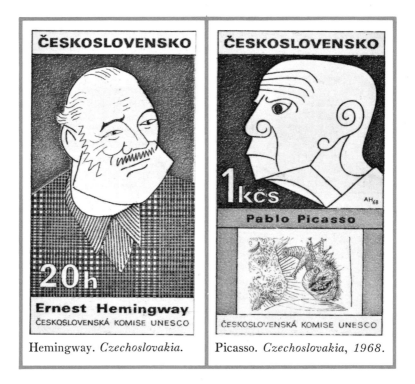

Hemingway. *Czechoslovakia.*

Picasso. *Czechoslovakia, 1968.*

Ernest Hemingway (1899-1961)

During the First World War the Illinois-born Hemingway was an ambulance driver in France and a soldier in the Italian infantry. His first short stories were hardly noticed, but in the 1920's he won fame as one of the leading members of the "lost generation" of Americans living abroad. He developed his tense, tough writing style as a war correspondent, and his novels glorify manliness and courage in the face of danger—at war, in bullfights, on big game hunts. His books, notably *The Old Man and the Sea*, won him the 1954 Nobel Prize in Literature. Hemingway lived in Spain, Africa, and Cuba. In the summer of 1961, sick and unable to write, Hemingway shot himself in his mountain retreat in Sun Valley, Idaho.

Pablo Picasso (1881-   )

Picasso was born in Malaga, Spain. When he was thirteen his father, an art teacher, let him have a studio of his own, and at fifteen he was accepted at art school in Barcelona, a city filled with the rich treasures of Catalan and Spanish art. Since 1904 Picasso has lived mostly in France. In Paris he absorbed the historic traditions of Northern European art as well as the exciting style of African sculpture. He has tried out every technique and worked in every medium. With the painter Braque he worked out a startling, abstract method of painting solid objects without destroying the flatness of the painting's surface. They called it Cubism. Picasso's most famous work, the mural "Guernica" (1937), testifies to his hatred of violence and war.

Chaplin. *Czechoslovakia, 1968.*   Disney. *United States, 1968.*

Charles Chaplin (1889-   )

Charlie Chaplin's father, a poor English actor, died young, and his sick mother was often in the hospital. At eight Chaplin was appearing regularly in London music halls, and later joined a pantomime troupe that toured the United States in 1913. The famous Hollywood director Mack Sennett hired Chaplin, who appeared in hilarious one and two-reel silent comedies as an unforgettable tramp with a tiny mustache, baggy pants, big shoes, and derby hat. Soon Chaplin was writing script and music, producing, directing, and acting in his own films, classics like *The Kid*, *Shoulder Arms*, *The Gold Rush*, and his first "talkie," *The Great Dictator*. Chaplin, who is married to Eugene O'Neill's daughter, now lives in Switzerland.

Walt Disney (1901-1966)

Disney was raised on a Missouri farm. After driving an ambulance in the First World War he went to art school in Chicago and started working as a commercial artist and cartoonist. In 1923 he began making films in Hollywood, and a few years later won fame with Mickey Mouse. He spoke Mickey's voice himself. Disney made *Snow White and the Seven Dwarfs*, the first full-length color cartoon, in 1938. Disney studio artists created both short and feature cartoons starring such beloved characters as Mickey, Donald Duck, Goofy, and Dumbo. After 1950 Disney produced a series of fascinating nature and adventure documentaries. In 1955 he opened his California amusement park, Disneyland.

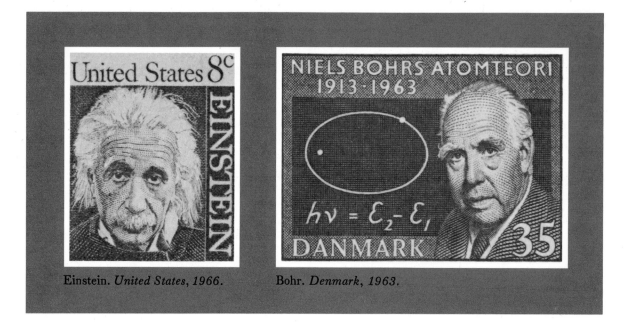

Einstein. *United States, 1966.*   Bohr. *Denmark, 1963.*

Albert Einstein (1879-1955)

Einstein was born at Ulm, Germany. He was slow to walk and talk, and at school in Munich he was considered a poor student. He finished his education in Switzerland and went to work as an examiner in the Swiss Patent Office. There he published his first original papers on theoretical physics and began to formulate his theory of relativity. In 1909 a special professorship was created for him at Zürich. In 1914 he became a professor at the University of Berlin and director of the Kaiser Wilhelm Institute. He received the Nobel Prize in Physics in 1921.

In the 1930's Hitler's anti-Jewish measures drove many of Germany's finest scientists, scholars, musicians, writers, and artists abroad, and Einstein was among them. After lecturing in England he settled in Princeton, New Jersey, in 1934 and became a professor at the university and an American citizen. Einstein brought with him the crucial formula that was the key to the atom-splitting experiments that converted matter into energy. In 1939 he wrote President Roosevelt that it would be possible to build a bomb based on atomic fission, and that Germany might very well build the bomb first. The atomic bomb was, of course, developed in the United States, and the Second World War ended in victory for the Allies. After the war Einstein recognized the unprecedented danger of such devices to mankind and called for international control of atomic weapons.

□   □   □

Niels Henrik David Bohr (1885-1962)

Bohr, a Copenhagen physicist, won a Nobel Prize in 1922 for his concept of the structure of the atom, which he reconciled with Einstein's quantum theory. He asserted that the atom consists of a system of electrons that rotate in orbits around a nucleus. Shortly before the Second World War Bohr told American scientists that he believed the uranium atom could be split into approximate halves. He returned to Denmark but fled the Nazis in 1943 and assisted in the development of the atom bomb at Los Alamos.

Sir Winston Churchill (1874-1965)

Churchill was born in Blenheim Palace, home of his grandfather, the Duke of Marlborough. His mother was an American heiress. He did badly in school, although even as a boy he felt a deep love for the English language. He passed the examination for military college only on his third try. As a young officer he fought briefly in India and the Sudan, and as a journalist he was taken prisoner in South Africa during the Boer War. He made a daring escape, and on his return to England he decided to make a career in politics. In 1900 he was elected to Parliament.

His political career had many ups and downs, and more than once he seemed "finished." Then, in May of 1940, Churchill became Prime Minister of Great Britain. Most of Europe had fallen to Hitler's armies, and England, short of men and airplanes and fearing invasion, faced Nazi Germany alone. When the blitz began Churchill himself tramped through the ruins as soon as the bombers had passed, rallying his people with fingers raised in his famous V-for-victory gesture. Over the radio he called for "victory at all costs, victory in spite of all terror." The Battle of Britain did end in victory against tremendous odds as the incredible morale of the English people held fast.

Churchill was swept out of office in the summer of 1945 but was subsequently chosen to serve again as Prime Minister. In 1946, in a speech he made in the United States, he originated the historic term "iron curtain." A sportsman and an amateur painter of exceptional skill, Winston Churchill won the 1953 Nobel Prize for Literature for books that included the six-volume *The Second World War* and *A History of the English-Speaking Peoples*. He was always proud of his American ancestry, and on a gray January day in 1965, at his funeral in St. Paul's Cathedral in London, the choir sang one of his favorites: "The Battle Hymn of the Republic."

Churchill. *United States, 1965.*

Eleanor Roosevelt (1884-1962)

Anna Eleanor Roosevelt, a niece of President Theodore Roosevelt, was the wife of President Franklin Delano Roosevelt. Her childhood was lonely—she was tall and shy, and she worried because she was neither dainty nor pretty. But she had a warm and sympathetic spirit, and with considerable effort she overcame her timidity and nervousness under the pressure of public life. The mother of five children, she cared for her husband after he was stricken with polio in 1921 and became his trusted adviser as he advanced from the governorship of New York to the presidency.

As First Lady Mrs. Roosevelt lectured, wrote a daily newspaper column, and traveled all over the world. After President Roosevelt died, in 1945 just before the end of the war in Europe, she helped to found the United Nations. She served as a United States delegate to the General Assembly and as Chairman of the Commission on Human Rights until 1952. Although she had been born to wealth and social position she chose to devote her life to progress, justice, and world peace and understanding. Her memoirs reflect her sensitivity and compassion as well as her remarkable energy and personal courage.

George Catlett Marshall (1880-1959)

This career army officer and statesman was born in Pennsylvania. He was a staff officer in the First World War and served in China in the 1920's. Chief of Staff of the United States Army in World War II, Marshall became General of the Army, or "five-star general," in 1944. After the war, as special representative of President Truman, he tried to set up a compromise government in war-torn China. In 1947 he became Secretary of State.

In a speech at Harvard in June, 1947, Marshall announced his imaginative cooperative program for American aid to devastated Europe, the European Recovery Program, commonly called the Marshall Plan. The United States was to contribute or loan money, machinery, raw materials, and technological advice (eventually amounting to twelve billion dollars' worth). The nations of Europe were to help each other wherever possible and trade more freely among themselves. By September sixteen nations adopted the four-year plan, although Russia and her satellites refused to take part. By 1951 the farms and factories of Western Europe had achieved the highest level of production in their history. In 1953 Marshall was honored with the Nobel Peace Prize.

Eleanor Roosevelt. *United States, 1963.*

Marshall. *United States, 1967.*

Pope John XXIII. *Spain, 1962.*   Hammarskjold. *United States, 1962.*

Pope John XXIII (1881-1963)

Pope John, who came of North Italian peasant stock, was born Angelo Roncalli. He served as a chaplain and medical corpsman in the First World War, as apostolic delegate to several Balkan countries, and as papal representative to liberated France in 1944. In 1953 he became Patriarch of Venice and in 1958 he was elected Pope. He was then seventy-seven years old. The new Pope's manner was surprisingly informal, and he had a warm, unpretentious personality. He often left the Vatican to visit the prisons and hospitals of Rome and talk with the people.

Pope John was deeply concerned about the divisions within the Christian faith, and he deplored the atheism, poverty, and illiteracy of modern times. He stunned the world by summoning the Second Vatican Council, which assembled in Rome in 1962 to revitalize the Church and bring it up to date to face the problems of the 20th Century. Councils had always been called only in extraordinary circumstances, and there had been only twenty of them in the entire history of the Church.

For the first time observers from Protestant and Orthodox denominations were invited. Within a few years major revisions in Church law and practice have been put into effect through the influence of the humble and humane "Pope of Peace."

Dag Hammarskjöld (1905-1961)

Hammarskjöld was a member of a distinguished Swedish family of scholars and statesmen. He was a monetary expert and served as chairman of the board of the Bank of Sweden. As a member of the Swedish foreign ministry he was often a delegate to international conferences, and in 1953 he became Secretary General of the United Nations. He traveled extensively and often stepped in personally to help settle disputes. A brilliant and meditative person, he was a poet and translator as well as a diplomat. While on a peace mission to the Congo in September, 1961, Hammarskjöld was killed in a tragic plane crash. He was awarded the 1961 Nobel Peace Prize after his death.

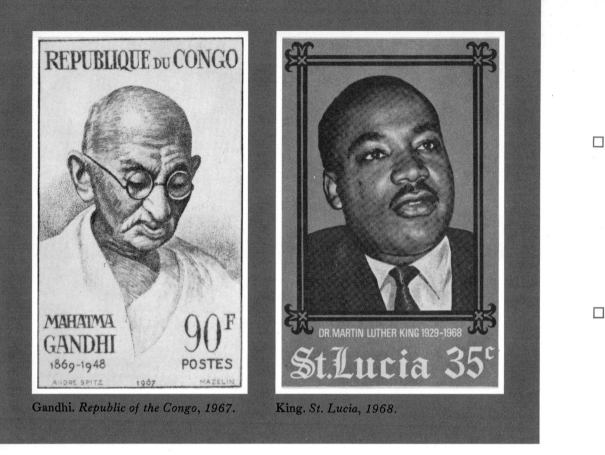

REPUBLIQUE DU CONGO

MAHATMA GANDHI 1869-1948 90F POSTES
ANDRE SPITZ 1967 MAZELIN

DR. MARTIN LUTHER KING 1929-1968

St.Lucia 35c

Gandhi. *Republic of the Congo, 1967.*   King. *St. Lucia, 1968.*

Mohandas K. Gandhi (1869-1948)

Gandhi, leader in India's struggle for independence, studied law in London and helped fight for civil rights for the thousands of Indians who lived in South Africa. On his return to India in 1915 he gave up western ways and led a life of abstinence. He wore the *khadi*, a simple homespun garment. Soft-spoken and deeply religious, Gandhi guided India towards the abolition of her rigid caste system. He believed in the unity of all men under one God and preached from Christian and Moslem Scriptures and the writings of Thoreau and Tolstoy as well as from the Hindu epics. Gandhi had great affection for Britain, but he refused to comply with British laws and policies he considered unjust. He knew that change was unavoidable, but he realized also that mankind had a choice between violent revolution and non-violent evolution. He called his form of passive resistance "truthforce." He was jailed by the British many times, and during one term in jail he read Thoreau's pamphlet "Civil Disobedience."

The people of India called Gandhi "Mahatma," or "Great Soul," and he won political concessions by fasting. He took part in conferences on Indian independence in 1947 but he was grieved by the religious rioting that led to the separation of Hindu India and Moslem Pakistan. Gandhi was assassinated in 1948 by a fellow Hindu who blamed him for the partition.

Martin Luther King, Jr. (1929-1968)

In 1955-56 a young Baptist minister in segregationist Montgomery, Alabama, led a boycott of the city buses in support of a poor Negro seamstress who had been too tired to give up her seat to a white person. It was the first of many protests, marches, and sit-ins led by Dr. King, who became head of the Southern Christian Leadership Conference in Atlanta. His tactics forced Congress to enact strong new laws that promise equal rights, opportunities, schooling, and jobs for black Americans. Dr. King, who won the 1964 Nobel Peace Prize, urged people to overcome violence and oppression through non-violence. Marchers sang "We Shall Overcome," and most Americans looked forward to the realization of King's dream of true brotherhood. In the face of threats to his family and bombings of his home Dr. King remained calm—he spoke occasionally about the possibility of sudden death. On the evening of April 4, 1968, as he stood talking with friends in Memphis, Dr. King was shot and killed.

John F. Kennedy (1917-1963)

John Fitzgerald Kennedy was the second of nine children in a wealthy Irish-American family from Massachusetts. He entered politics to fulfill the ambitions of his older brother, who had been killed in the Second World War. A navy hero and Pulitzer-Prize-winning author, he served in both houses of Congress before winning the presidency in 1960 in a close election. The handsome, scholarly President urged new civil rights laws and aid to education, and set up the Peace Corps and the Alliance for Progress in Latin America. He guided the nation through crises in Berlin and Cuba, won Congressional approval for Project Apollo, and worked with the Soviet Union toward a nuclear test ban agreement. Kennedy was the youngest elected President of the United States, the first Roman Catholic, and the first to be born in the 20th Century. After only a thousand days in office he was assassinated in Dallas, on November 22, 1963, and on that day of tragedy Kennedy became the youngest of our presidents to die.

□

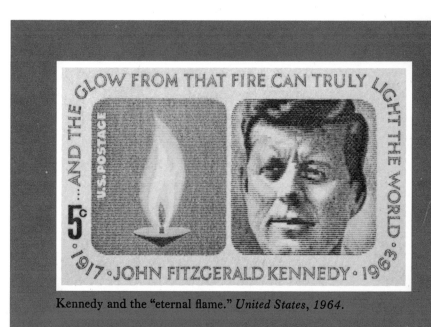

Kennedy and the "eternal flame." *United States, 1964.*

INDEX